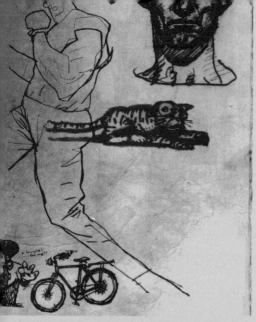

VASA A GOGO

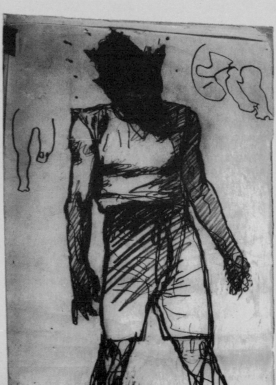

*art & collaborations*

# RICK BERRY & PHIL HALE

DONALD M. GRANT, PUBLISHER, INC.

# d o u b l e

# m e m o r y

*I thought you were confused, but I was confused*

*Designer: Phil Hale / Project Managers: the Berrys*

Grateful acknowledgement is made
for permission to reprint quotes from the following:

page 13—Antonio Carlos Jobim from *Nobody's Angel*
by Thomas McGuane © 1982 Random House, Inc.

page 41—*Barbarous Coast*
by Ross Macdonald © 1990 Warner Books, Inc.

page 53—*Krazy Kat* by George Herriman
special permission © 1933 King Features Syndicate, Inc.

page 101—*Farewell My Lovely*
by Raymond Chandler © 1988 Random House, Inc.

Printed in Hong Kong through Interprint

Deluxe Edition  ISBN 1-880418-04-5
Trade Edition  ISBN 1-880418-05-3

FIRST EDITION

DONALD M. GRANT, PUBLISHER, INC.
HAMPTON FALLS, NEW HAMPSHIRE
0     3     8     4     4

*This book is for Sheila Berry*

This book couldn't have happened without the following people, and if it seems like a lot of people, that's because we needed a lot of help.

*t  h  a  n  k  y  o  u*

Darrel Anderson, Joel Hagen, Ann Howland, Jeff Jones, George Milton, Mary & Bren Shiner, Frank & Teresa Vaughan and family, Robert K. Wiener, and Pete Wigens.

*a  c  k  n  o  w  l  e  d  g  e  m  e  n  t  s*

Jeff Anderson & family, Steve Bentley, Kaye & Phyllis Berry Jr., KL & Ann Berry, L.A.Berry, Jules "Whitey" Bigg, Roger Biles, Pop Boarman, Tom Canty, Eugene Dorgan, Chris & Eva, the Eidsons, Dana Frazee, Jack Frost, Archie Goodwin, Chris & Anne Hale, Mike & Jean-Marie Hale, Thomas Haber, Jim Higgins, Ron Hueftle, Kirk Kennedy, Thomas Kidd, Vincent McCaffrey, Clarissa Milton, Lisa Petrucci, Joanne & Claude Poirier, Stacy Quinn, Frank M. Robinson, Artie Romero, Bent Schmidt-Nielsen, David "Mister" Seeley, Marlene Silva, Lisa Tomlinson, Vooch, Lauren Walsh & her fifth graders, Jerry Wiest, Jon Wigens, Terry Windling, and all at AVH west.

*Some of the images in this book are the work of the publisher's mother.*

a Vasa a gogo

# CONTENTS

# OBLIGATO

my friends which art in art dreaming of the day when
their dreams into one neither a bang nor a whimper
but a sweet blending like a blue sky evening where you
cannot tell where the color changes

becomes something else the blue so pure I had the
same dream all the visions of hell and heaven
pummelled me not bruised but I was made not a little
sensitive to cry of the mind gnawing of the heart
drunkenness of a mule and all heard smelled
unending a rounded belief in scratching a

living out in the colours of love and loss oh yes I've
dreamed the same drunken dream epic epic in it's
smallness

make no claims for it they should glow (or die) with
their own each one to sink your eyes into some to smirk
at all to make a claim many-headed the poet the hack
the painter the eye single solo a belief in what the eye
can see what could be washed up on the shores
behind the eye not always sweet my friends bad and
wonderful and poised poised to go on believe in it all
believe that it makes a difference announce a small
truth a picture break the reverie now and you have a
truth a mad truth to discover.

*–George Milton*

Dreams. I feel them passionately. And, okay, that's fine, but dammit, I want to be *passionate*.

"To be honest with you," he says, "the artist that I am—the artist that I want to be—*is* that passion."

CONCHITA   OIL 1992 BERRY

FIGO DELLA MADONNA    OIL  1989  BERRY /HALE

CARYATID   OIL 1992 BERRY

4

CRUSH   OIL 1989 BERRY/HALE

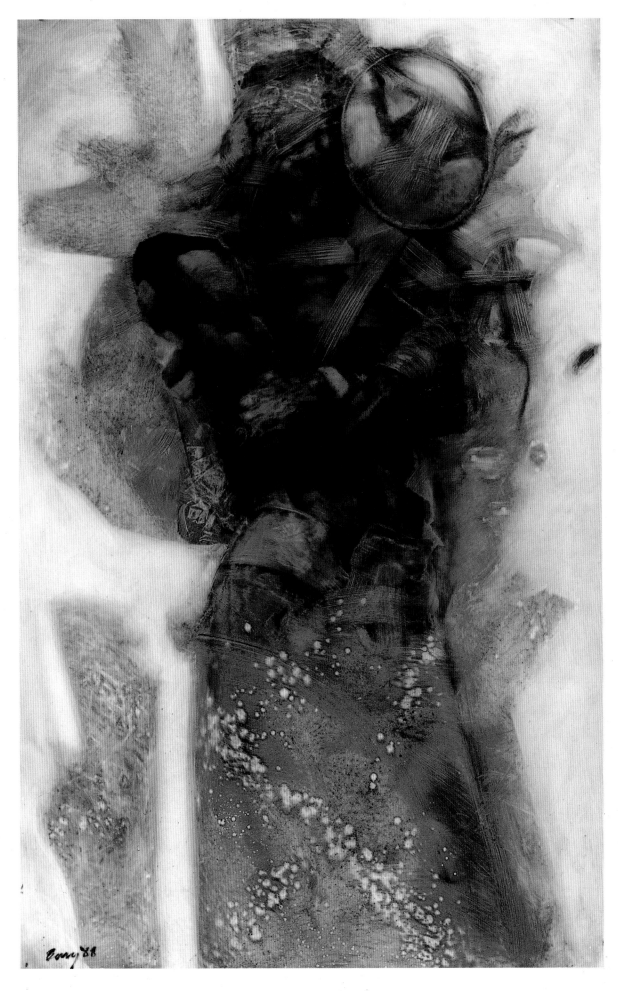

DRY SCIENCE   OIL 1987 BERRY

42ND & 8TH   OIL 1987 BERRY

THESE TINY FEET IN MY HEART    OIL  1988  HALE

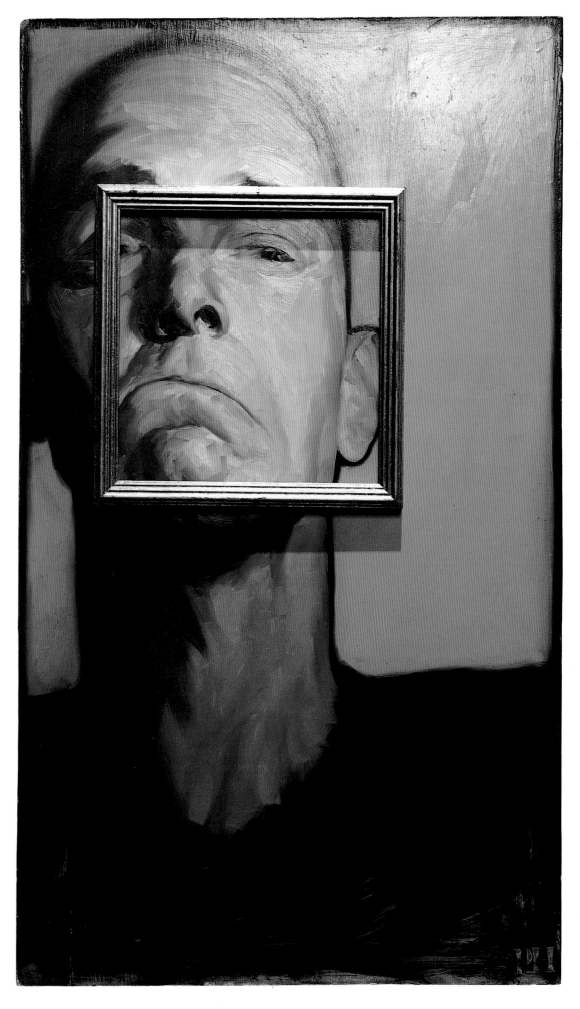

GUIGNOL'S BAND    OIL 1991   HALE

BELLING THE MOON    OIL  1992  BERRY

27 IS DYING   OIL 1992  BERRY

More often than not, the shortest distance between two points is cheating. Intangible and amorphous terms—truth, right—are easily suborned by the more containable queries of 'appropriate?' and 'will it fit?' This sort of ruthless self-examination is the spine of any attempt to make people give you their money.

cheating

"*I photographed you with my Rolleiflex.
It showed your enormous ingratitude.*"

— Antonio Carlos Jobim

HEAD   1991  HALE  *(with Rick)*

14

WAITING FOR THE LATE NIGHT FRIEND    1992   HALE

PIG TANGO   1992  HALE

SCISSOR-CUT PIE   1992  HALE

INSECT-HEADED MAN

1

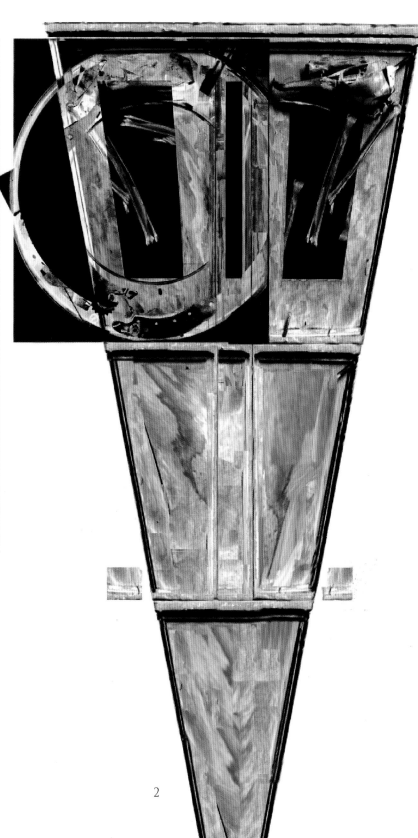

2

1  INSECT-HEADED MAN    1992  HALE  *(with Rick)*

2  DOUBLE MEMORY    1992  HALE

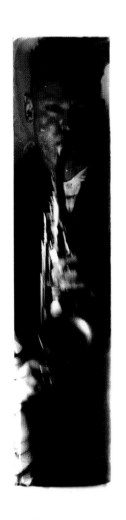

BLURT   1991   HALE

THE CUBAN HEELS   OIL  1991  HALE

NEARLY WHITE   1992   HALE

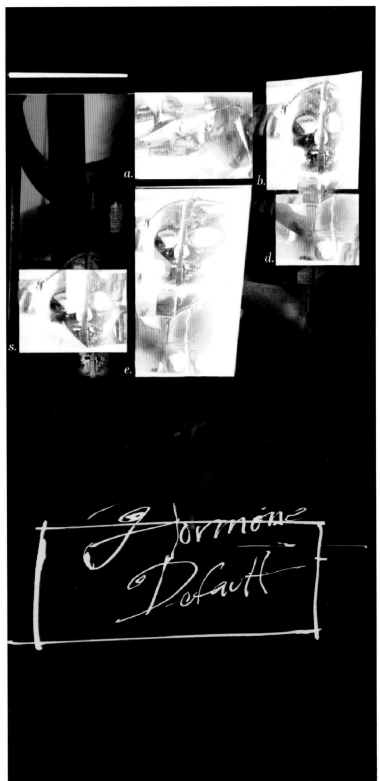

HORMONE DEFAULT   1992   HALE

BLOTTER   1992  BERRY/BERRY  *(with Phil)*

BLOWROD   1992   HALE

'Pigment-hurlinga': the sweet distillation, informed by that sly camber of logic, by the allegorical limbs which pepper the face of the piece. Easily (almost contemptuously), the artist gives leash to his sense of 'fun', now chattering like freezing rain over the plodding umber of the ground, now the master technician. The gesture itself, vivid and near-autographic, would seem reason enough (the twangy promise of a light bulb, the earthy smell of sidewalk night). Berry often seems as confused by his choices as we are.

"The Berry world, 'Berryworld', a world where Gloria Steinem comforts Norman Mailer over the failure of his muffins, a palette restricted by early-color-TV."

And all of this (only the most cosmetic of chainsaws) were it not for his understated dualism, paralleled with the Mr. Berry's reliance on the observer's willingness to self-reference is as charming as his reluctance to 'finish' his paintings. The pieces remain volatile even as he annotates the often painful distinction between memory and experience. But what an experience! Even the most casual of examinations instantly rewards the viewer; background, foreground, brown, blue, the artist impregnates the surface of the piece with hints and goads, a cartographic malice, a thesian cord to the crisis of intent which electrifies the early portrait-like 'personals'— transparent bone rising day-glo ascent through the successive skins of paint, gradually structured through alternating layers of wash and impasto (thick as butter) hanging in giddy suspension over a more ambiguously driven 'maybe' or 'perhaps' area, an approach the artist engagingly redefines as "Seduced and Abandoned".

No. The strength of these pieces lies not so much in their accuracy or absolute vindication as in their refusal to be judged by these same standards.

*"...holes bored through their arms and bodies and had feet shaped like a pie, I was filled with emotion."*

— Mark Twain

THE MARRIAGEABLE WOMAN   OIL 1985  BERRY

THE HERALD   OIL 1986  BERRY

TINY BED OF DREAMS   OIL  1992  BERRY

THREE WITCHES   OIL/DIGITAL  1985  BERRY

26

HATCHECK  OIL 1992 BERRY

NEMESIS  OIL  1990  BERRY

THREE FATES OIL 1985 BERRY

THE BAPTIST  OIL  1990  BERRY

SHAMAN   OIL 1988  BERRY

A philosophy as a miracle of reduction, a triumph of simplification and commitment over everything that is ambiguous about the world. Insatiable appetites and brutal meat converge in sinister alignment. A juggler struggles with a single ball.

"*I was fresh, I was full-bodied, I was flavoursome. In my mind I was naked.*"

COMING TO GRIEF   OIL 1992   HALE

LOS VASCOS   OIL   1992   HALE

35

SUNDAY AT NOON   OIL  1992  HALE

36

EN FLAGRANTE   OIL 1992  HALE

NO VENTURE NO FREUD *(sketch)* OIL 1992 HALF

INDELICATO *(sketch)* OIL 1992 HALE

38

DESTINY INSISTS   OIL 1992 HALE

A man's obligations don't end at his fingertips, and you can't be proud all the time. The future, the past, they can swing at your neck like a dead bird, the demands of a thousand thousand nights can jam in your veins while you scream like a polyglot. And there's no shame in that, but it takes more than hope to float your wallet. Still, life has it's measure of good times as well. Brilliant chinese clouds, the same sky, a succession of faces open in the breeze. With every step somebody else bends over backwards to do it again and drowns in the mud, martyr butterflies.

"Imagine if you will," he says, the first tentative invectives (J'accuse perhaps), "I find my legs and use them, the door, now an object of surest utility. Sibling-like, I kiss her. And am rewarded: her arms describe me in yard-long swipes."

In this sort of context privacy becomes a relative term and a working knowledge of careful is your pal. The truth may scare you, but it's smaller than you are and late at night.

*"I think you're exciting," she said in an unexcited way.*

—Ross Macdonald

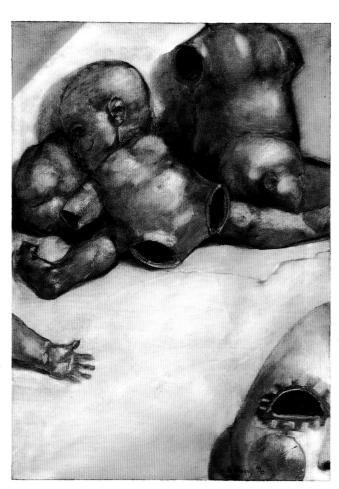

NEMESIS QUARTET OIL 1990 BERRY

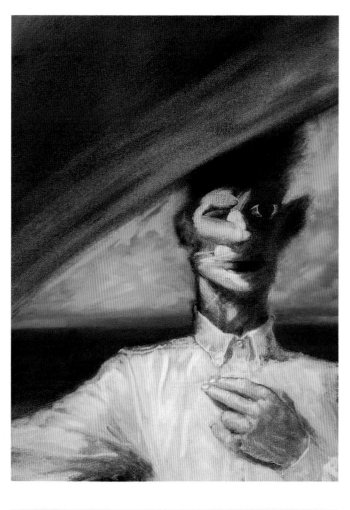

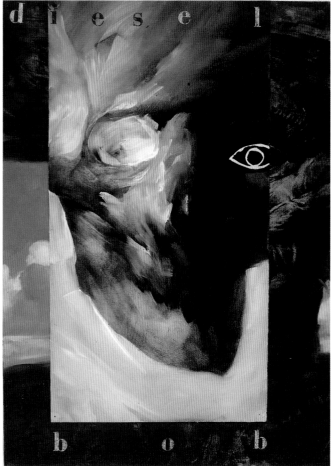

THE WHIPPING BOYS   OIL  1991  BERRY/HALE

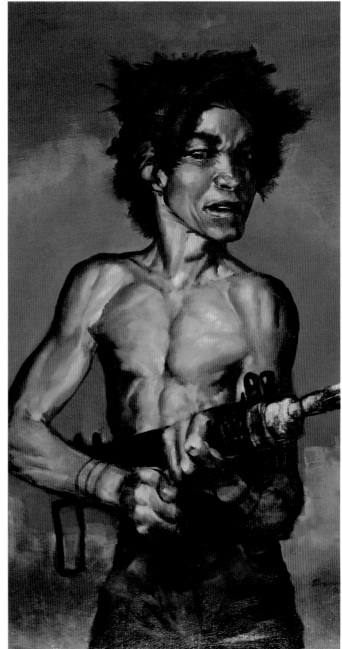

ELROY   OIL 1984 BERRY/HALE

JACK *(sketch)*   OIL 1984 BERRY

COUNTING THE WAYS   OIL  1988  HALE

45

CROUCH END   OIL  1984  HALE

ROLAND   OIL  1986  HALE

46

AMATEUR  OIL  1988  HALE          A DISTANT GLORY   OIL  1992  BERRY

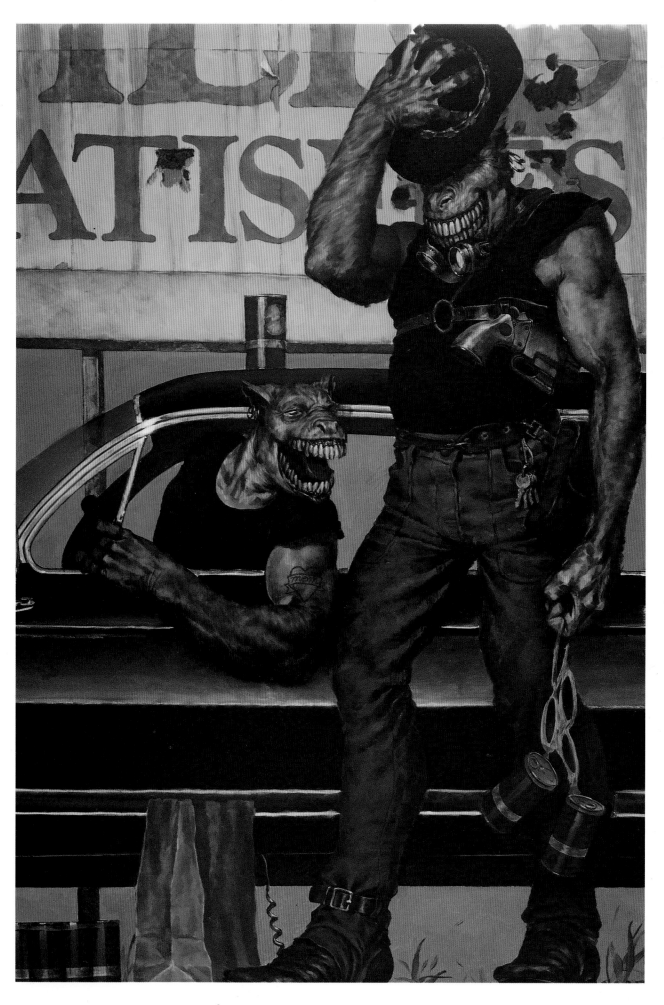

SATISFACTION   OIL 1984 HALE

NAKED RAYGUN   OIL 1988 HALE

NIGHTCHARGER   OIL  1987   BERRY

COVENANT   OIL 1988  BERRY

*p    i    e    -    c    u    t        e    y    e*

The unaesthetic line. You don't owe it a thing. And there's
more: it's virtues and failings are so nearly the same that even
the most dismal of efforts can move into realms of glory.

"*And there he is with brick — hostile reptile*"
—George Herriman

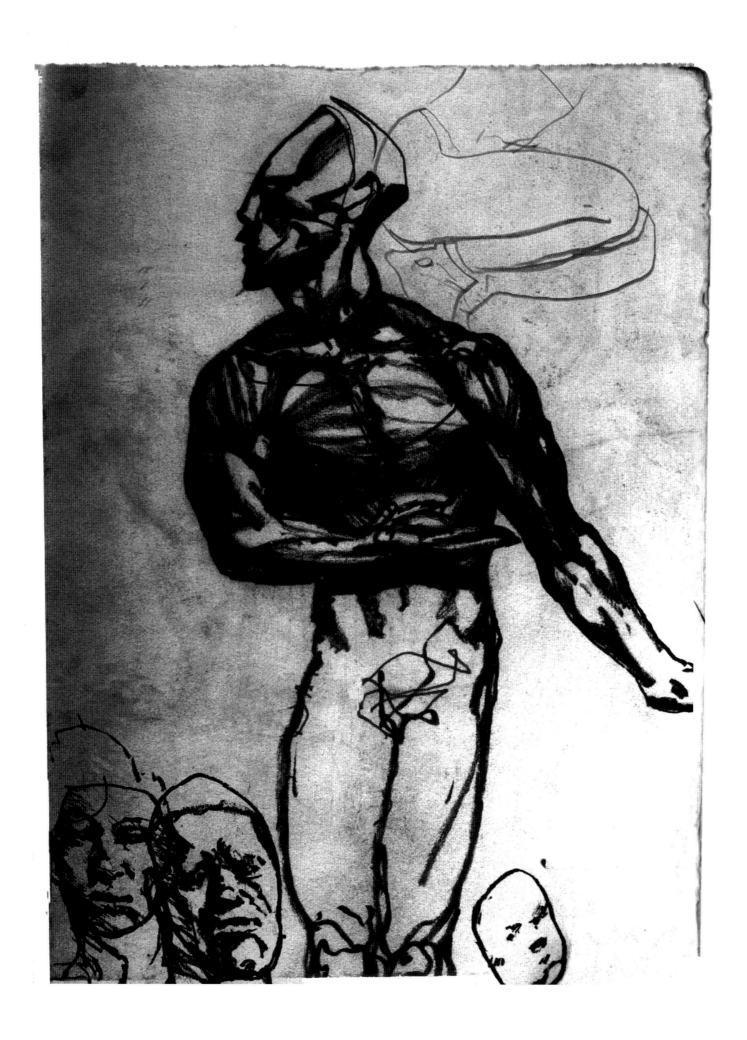

56

58

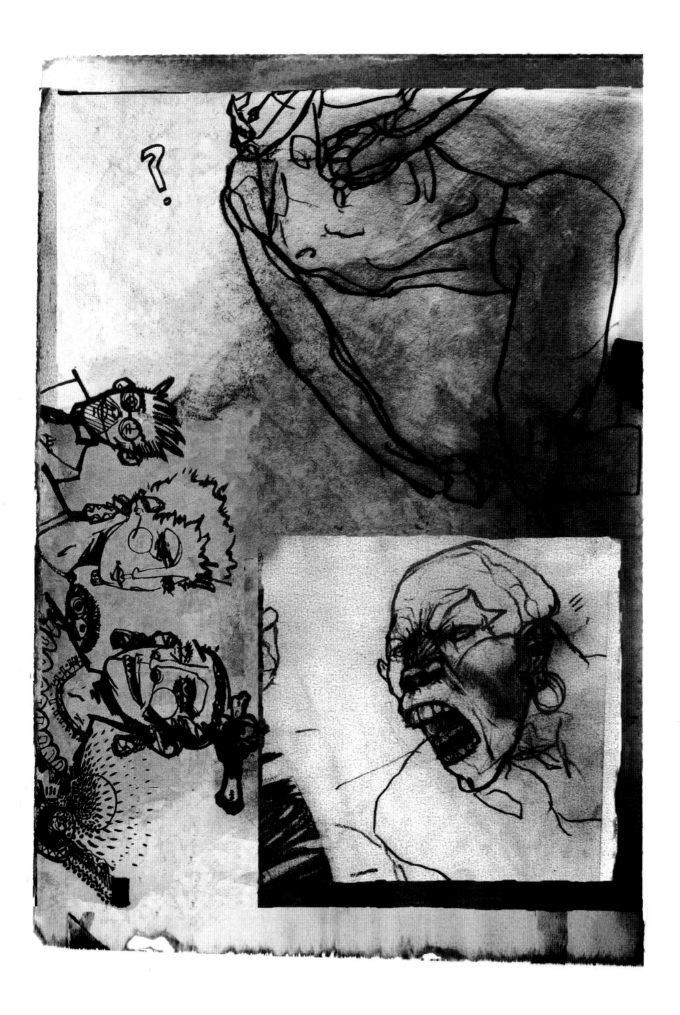

63

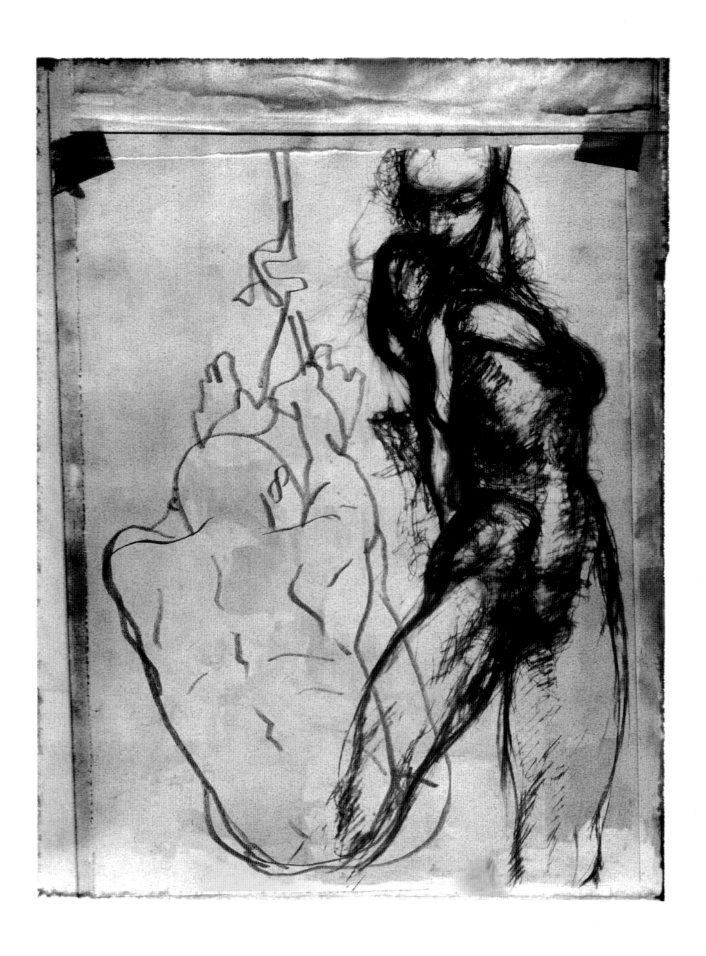

PG

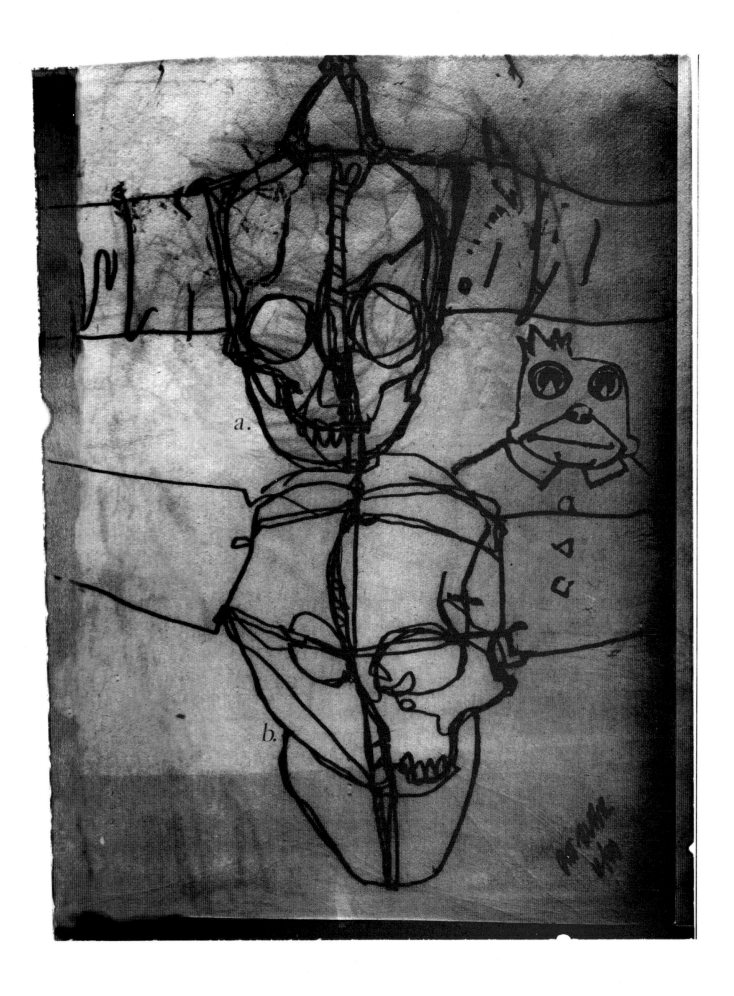

a.

b.

79

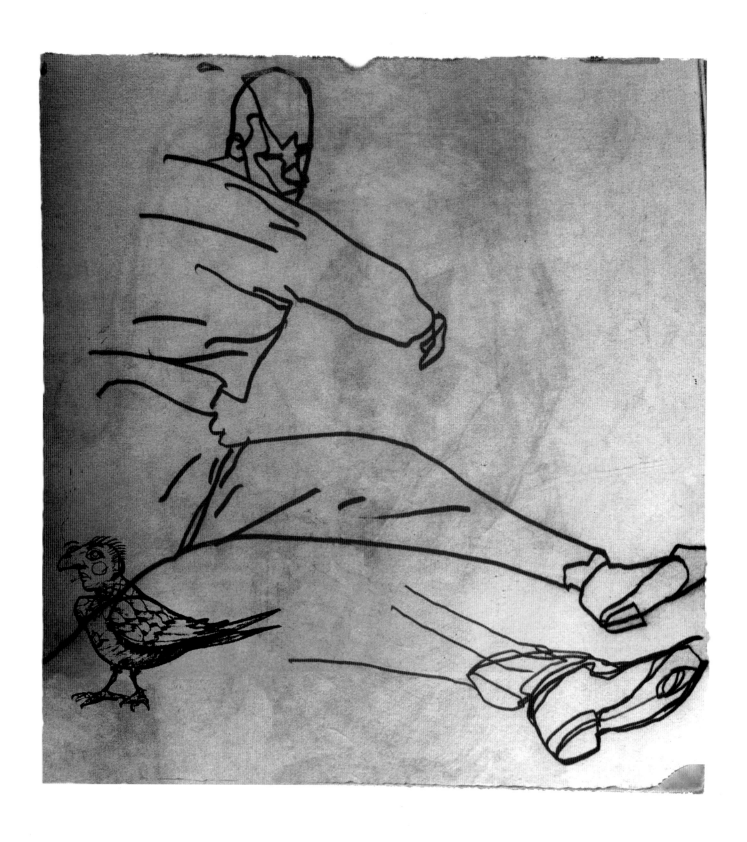

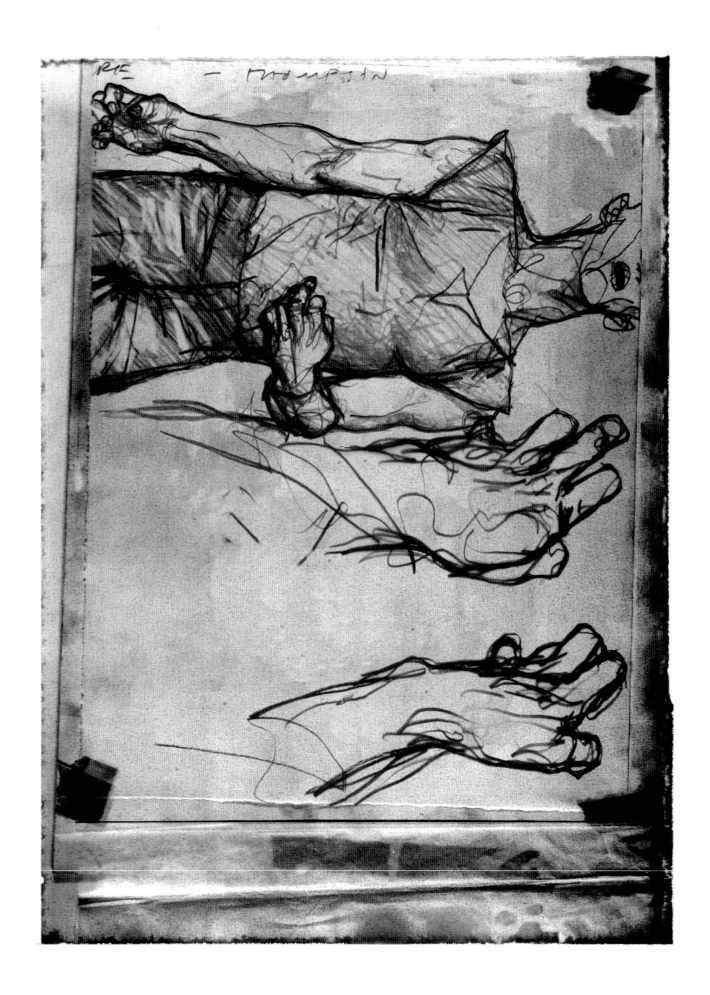

82

EN FLAGRANTE

perfect blue day

The twentieth century, long lost to the reverse haircuts of progress,  has not been altogether kind to various talents: a man that can repeatedly peg a moving target with a household object no longer strikes the proud profile a more appreciative era would have fitted to him. This is a story Mr. Berry has had to endure for a lifetime.

And this story cannot be compromised. It does not have a 'negative capacity', or 'work as a shuffle'. It holds to the clean lines of annoying, where it's job is declared. And that job is:

However you work to avoid it, there inevitably arrives that damning pause where whole truths will make themselves entirely comprehensible to you: liking what you do and getting paid for it aren't necessarily the same thing.

Put another way, this is not always the same thing as art. This is often commercial art. And while art is about pleasing yourself, commercial art is about pleasing somebody else, a fundamental difference.

Mr Berry, fortunately, is somebody else.

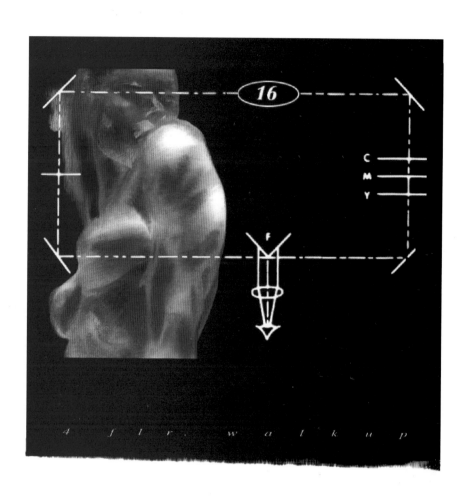

"*Chance reveals virtues and vices as light reveals objects.*"
—La Rochefoucauld

AT HOME WITH THE BACONS    OIL  1988  BERRY

TROUBLE WITH THE CAT *(with Hale)*   OIL  1988  BERRY

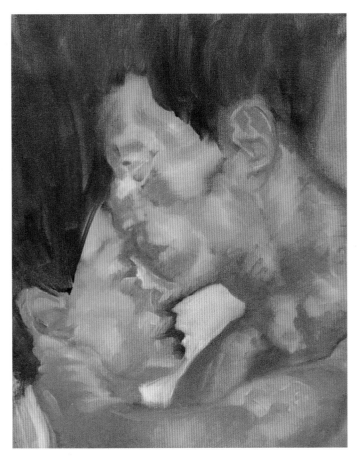

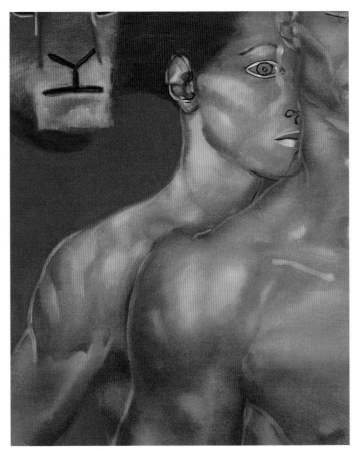

FOUR FROM 16   OIL  1988  BERRY

NINE ROOMS   OIL   1988   BERRY

91

" The surface transient, a fluid yielding collapse of dimming
light, a shimmering silvery elusive regret, it refuses to become
fixed or visually realised. And beneath it, Half-Dreamed, Half-
Spoken, the ubiquitous fish (emblem of the human capacity to
probe the unconscious?).

An unchosen confrontation, Hale's work demands a sort of
aesthetic denial—the funky approximation of a pointing finger;
the sensuality of the surface betrayed by the non-colors the
artist referees. And yet, for all of the coy ephemereality, one can
still gouge oneself on the horns of his masterfully orchestrated
brushwork and stand naked, a twenty minute egg. "

Close on the heels of 16. A conscious effort to back out of the
dead-end of technique and move towards something with more
immediacy and bang. Illustration generally requires knowing
what you're going to get, and knowing what you're going to get
is, every day, a little death. A refined and consistent approach
and a preordained end result are two lines intersecting on gray
pork boredom. The expedient completion of mechanical
procedure is it's own exquisite reward, but finish oriented
technique can leave you with nowhere to go, and eventually a
man must recognize the flimse and heave of failure in his tree
brush, his sky brush, his lip brush, and beg for what he already
has.

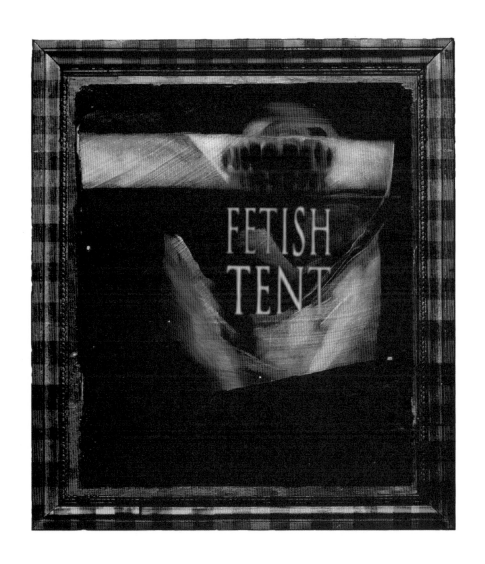

*"As our character deteriorates, so does our taste."*
—La Rochefoucauld

KINDLE   OIL  1988  HALE                    LOSING THEORY   OIL  1988  HALE

94

GAG  OIL  1988  HALE

THE CIGARETTE-PUNCH   OIL 1988 BERRY

THOUGHTLESS   OIL 1992 BERRY

EVERY NIGHT   OIL 1988 HALE

SO NOW YOU KNOW   OIL 1992 BERRY

THE BLIND BOXERS   OIL  1988  MILTON

SIDEWAYS   OIL  1988  HALE

COPPERHEAD   MIXED MEDIA  1988  HALE

CLOSE OIL 1988 HALE

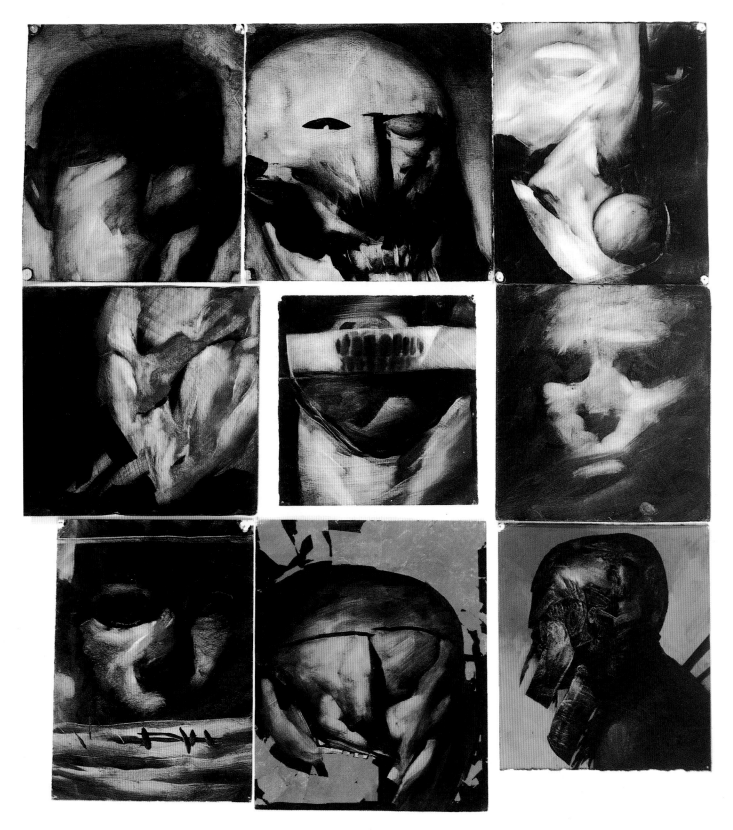

FETISH STACK  OIL  1989  HALE

Impetuous, playful, by turns sober and enigmatic, the boys know which way is up. Twelve years is a long time, they've run out of fingers, and a hungry future squats on the horizon. They are happy frogs in a dynamite pond: a compelling vindication of all that is fine and decent about this beautiful country.

Phil, once a youthful two-thirds of Rick's age, now approaches three-quarters; Rick has now figured in close on a third of Phil's life. Phil appears in over a quarter of Rick's, but he will never catch up. Mathematics, however, have played a conventional role in the friendship; now well over a decade of can-do and know-how, collaboration and ha-ha.

Those early pre-visual days, a starting point: they quickly achieve a purposeless tension and stay there, mutilating backyard polaroids with a ball-point pen, the combined low-motor-skill and gutter-standard exciting in the viewer a wealth of pity and discomfort. Soon modest fantasies of four color reproduction reduce any art director to inert good looks divided by tears. Already collaboration is across the board, automatic, the crux of the relationship: the whole shebang. Unusable and contradictory insights compel them towards the direst of stupidities. Attributing authorship becomes tedious and somewhat besides the point. Styles and appropriations become so thoroughly tangled, cribbed, so influenced and counter-influenced that a listing of paintings can be read like a conversation. And in parallel evolution, the terms: the freehand bodge, the double-hand and the double-bench; each choice affirmed by the singularity of the *patois*, a complicated failure of hair and brain.

They work into the wet paint, these near-kings of colored paste, they don't care—side by side they address the canvas in a moment as unmarred by sentimentality as the effortless sweep of the crenolated sea.

"*It was a nice walk, if you like grunting.*"
—Raymond Chandler

ORPHEUS DENIED   OIL  1991  HALE

THE ATAVIST   OIL 1992  HALE

GYMNAST   OIL 1989 BERRY

ELEANOR  OIL  1992  BERRY

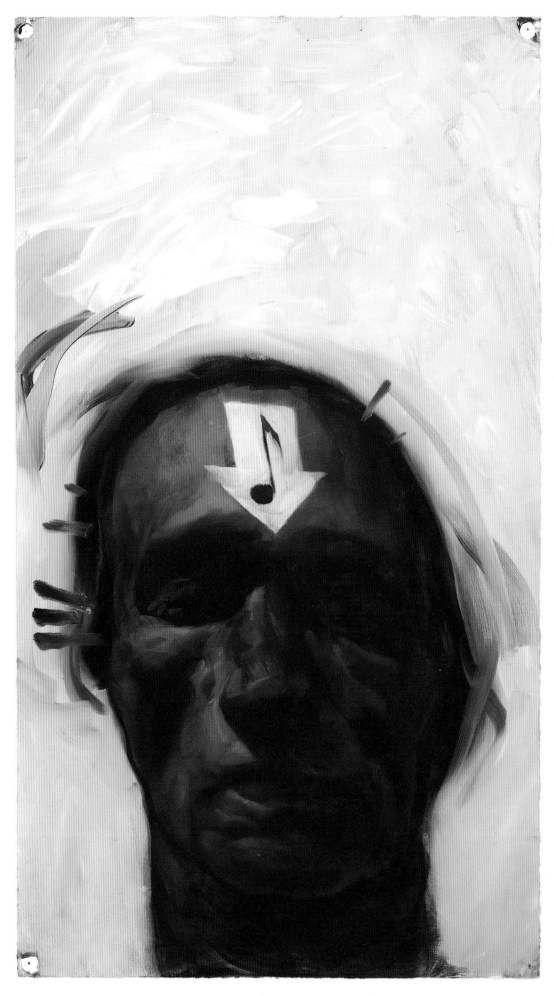

DOUG, DOUG, THE MUSICAL SLUG  OIL  1992  HALE

OUTCAST   OIL  1990  BERRY

STROLL THROUGH THE TOMB   OIL 1989 BERRY

POST OAKS AND SAND ROUGHS   MIXED MEDIA 1988  HALE

THE WEEPING SONG   OIL   1989   BERRY/HALE

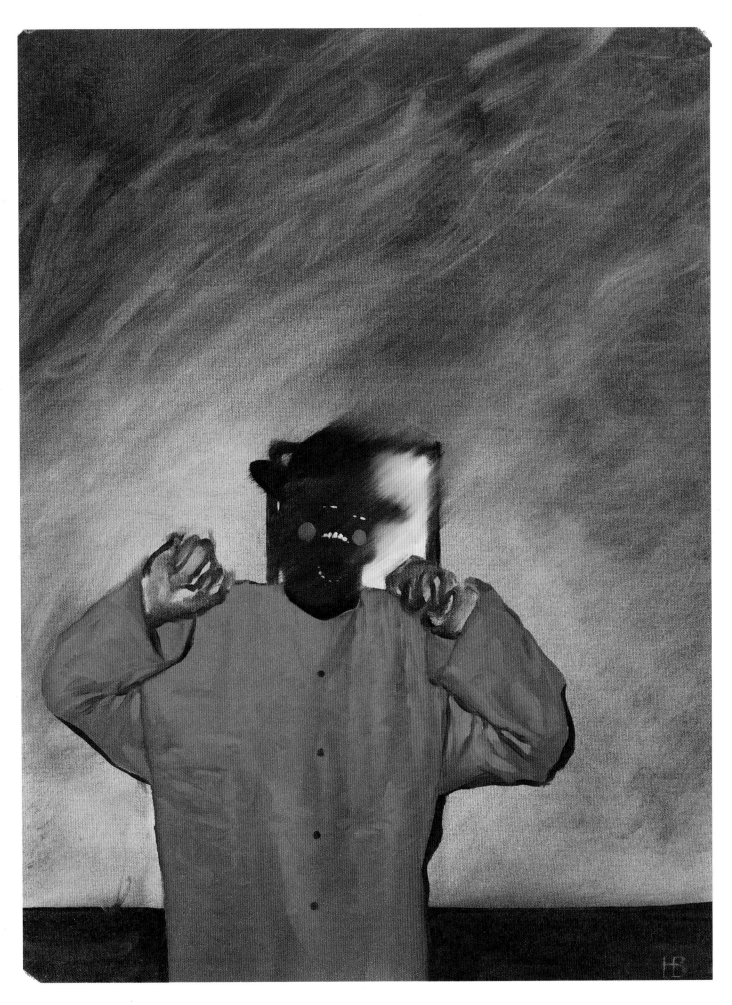

BECOMING THE FRICTIONAL   OIL 1988  HALE

AMERICAN CRIME   OIL  1985  BERRY

EVERYBODY WANTED HIM TO STOP   OIL  1988  HALE

HOSTAGE   OIL 1985 BERRY

114

MOROCCO   OIL 1989 BERRY

117

*c o l o p h o n*

This book was set in Bauer-Bodoni, Times, and Trajan.

Composed by *a vasa a go/go* on a Macintosh 2fx using Adobe Photoshop and Quark Xpress.

The best of the reproduction photography by *Richard Kiely*.

Digital file references produced by *Zoom Photo*.

Print liason : *Interprint*

The music of *Nick Cave and the Bad Seeds* had a powerful effect upon the authors during production.

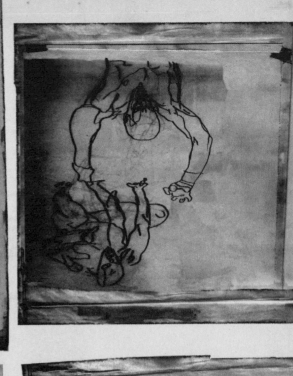

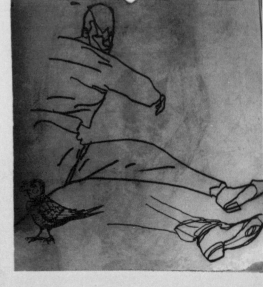